SHEPHERDS AND
SHEPHERDING

Jonathan Brown

SHIRE PUBLICATIONS

SHIRE PUBLICATIONS
Bloomsbury Publishing Plc

PO Box 883, Oxford, OX1 9PL, UK
1385 Broadway, 5th Floor, New York, NY 10018, USA
Email: shire@bloomsbury.com
www.shirebooks.co.uk

© 2013 Jonathan Brown.

First published 2013
Transferred to digital print on demand 2018

A CIP catalogue record for this book is available from the
British Library.

Shire Library no. 732
ISBN-13: 978 0 74781 226 5

Jonathan Brown has asserted his right under the
Copyright, Designs and Patents Act, 1988, to be
identified as the author of this book.

Designed by Tony Truscott Designs, Sussex, UK
Typeset in Perpetua and Gill Sans
Printed and bound in Great Britain.

COVER IMAGE
A Cotswolds shepherd and one of his lambs, a photograph
taken by John Tarlton.

TITLE PAGE IMAGE
Gathering a stray sheep, from an Edwardian postcard.

CONTENTS PAGE IMAGE
Driving a flock across a Cheshire hillside, 2011.

ACKNOWLEDGEMENTS
All illustrations are from the Museum of English Rural Life
in Reading, except for those on the contents page and
page 33 (top).

Shire Publications is supporting the Woodland Trust, the UK's leading woodland conservation charity, by funding the dedication of trees.

CONTENTS

INTRODUCTION: SHEEP FARMING IN BRITAIN

A highland shepherd with his dogs and an orphan lamb wrapped in a sling, from a postcard of the early twentieth century.

SHEEP have been an important part of British farming for centuries. The income from sheep and wool paid for the building of many of the magnificent medieval churches of East Anglia, for example. Sheep have been kept in almost every district of Britain, from the fells and mountains of the north to the lowland pastures and mixed farming of the south. The different habitats of Romney Marsh, the Cotswolds, Exmoor and Dartmoor, the Lincolnshire Wolds, the Welsh mountains and the Cheviot hills have all been noted for their part in sheep husbandry, and have given their names to some of the breeds of sheep. For the contrasts between regions are considerable, leading to the need for types of sheep adapted to the different environments, and differences in the way they are managed. There are more than sixty distinct breeds of sheep in British farming, while a number of old breeds – the Berkshire Nott, for example – disappeared in the nineteenth century, superseded by newer types.

The keeping of sheep has been a constant feature of the farming scene: since statistics were first collected in the mid-nineteenth century the number of sheep in Great Britain has most of the time been within the range of 20–30 million. The main exceptions were during the two world wars, when sheep farming was discouraged, and there have been other periods of decline following epidemic diseases and some severe winters, such as 1947. However, sheep farming has not been unchanging. Even during the last two centuries, on which this book is focused, there have been many changes in the part sheep have played in farming. Sheep had been kept primarily for wool up to the eighteenth century, but by the end of the century their value for meat was becoming more appreciated. A century later, the market for wool was declining in the face of competition from imports, and it has continued ever since. Instead, mutton and,

The Cotswold breed of sheep as it was in the mid-nineteenth century, illustrated in David Low's book on British livestock breeds, published in 1842.

increasingly, lamb became the dominant products. In medieval times sheep were also kept for their milk; the late twentieth century has seen a revival of interest in ewe's milk.

Changing patterns of sheep farming have affected the breeds kept. Some types of sheep that produce high-quality wool, such as the Lincolnshire Longwool, have become rare breeds, replaced by others that capitalise on the sheep's potential as a producer of mutton and lamb. The geography of sheep-keeping has shifted as well. Sheep were kept in almost all types of farming in the mid-nineteenth century, but towards the end of the century changing patterns of farming led to a decline of sheep-keeping in the lowlands of the south and east of England. Sheep have not disappeared from these areas, but they are not kept so much on the chalk Downs, instead moving to the valleys, where they are fed on pasture. While numbers kept on the lowlands have declined, they have increased on hill farms in the north and west.

In July 1940 Mr J. E. Quested's pedigree Romney Marsh sheep were evacuated from his farm in the Isle of Thanet, Kent to somewhere further from the battle for Britain's skies. They were photographed being sorted and marked ready for the journey.

WHO WERE THE SHEPHERDS?

A MONG THE SUBJECTS favoured by photographers of country life in the late nineteenth and early twentieth centuries was the shepherd portrait. There he stands, lamb in one hand, crook in the other and dog at his feet, the picture of sturdiness, dependability and independence.

There was romance in some of these portraits of the 'shepherd of the hills'. He attracted literary attention as well, more than any other farm workers, more even than the horseman and ploughboy. Journalists and other writers of the late nineteenth and early twentieth centuries published their accounts of conversations with shepherds – examples of oral history before the term gained currency. Some of these books, such as W. H. Hudson's *A Shepherd's Life*, are classics, rarely out of print. The tradition has continued: the popularity of the television programme *One Man and His Dog* was one manifestation of the continuing interest in the shepherding life.

There was solid practical reality reflected in those portraits as well. Another classic of country literature, but of a different kind, W. Fream's textbook *The Elements of Agriculture* stated: 'The shepherd is a very important person on a sheep-breeding farm, and a shepherd who understands his duties, and can perform them efficiently, is a well-qualified man of sound experience.'

By most reckonings the shepherd was at the top of the tree of the workers on the farm. He was 'one of the choicest of rural men' according to a mid-nineteenth-century farming encyclopaedia. The nature of his work gave him the independence the photographers sought to portray. He was free to organize his own work most of the time. The foreman or bailiff had almost no influence over him; even the farmer had to defer sometimes. A. G. Street related the story of a shepherd on a farm near his own in Wiltshire who gave in his notice after the farmer did not consult him about selling a spare rick of hay. The farmer bought the rick back. Persuading the shepherd to leave his fields to help out at harvest time could require the utmost diplomacy on the part of the farmer. The shepherd would condescend to come 'for an hour or two', Street wrote, 'as one conferring a favour'.

Opposite: Farmer Frank Whatley started work as a shepherd boy aged ten. He had just turned ninety in 1947 when he was photographed posing in an old shepherd's smock, surrounded by his sheep on the Wiltshire Downs.

A timeless theme: this photograph of the shepherd and his dog could have been taken almost any time. It was in fact taken in the 1960s, of a shepherd in Dorset.

A shepherd takes his flock across a field of stubble, on which hens are grazing, in Hampshire in the 1930s.

The shepherd was in a position of great trust, having charge of the flock, spending long periods with little contact with his employer. This was especially marked in some regions. There were farmers in Lincolnshire, for example, who bred sheep on their main farm on the hills, but also had detached holdings on the lowland marshes, where shepherds were left to manage the flocks independently. In the uplands of Wales, northern England and Scotland the shepherd could spend weeks away with the flock grazing extensive hill pastures. Close contact with the sheep meant, naturally enough, that the shepherd took a proprietorial

interest in them – they were always 'my sheep', especially when they won prizes at agricultural shows. The shows in the border country are still called 'Shepherds' Shows'. In some areas, especially the northern uplands, such proprietorship had more substantial meaning. The shepherd's wage was not paid in cash, but in a share in the flock. Many a shepherd of Northumberland took his wages entirely in this form, others had part of their remuneration in kind. It was a form of employment that was declining during the second half of the nineteenth century, but was still to be found in the 1880s. Scottish shepherds were similarly paid almost entirely in kind, with quantities of oatmeal, potatoes and coal all contributing to their income; they were also allowed, even encouraged, to run a flock of their own together with their employer's. At the other end of the country another type of freelance arrangement saw the shepherds of Romney Marsh shared by a number of neighbouring farmers, and paid 1s 6d an acre.

The shepherd was among those farm workers hired on an annual contract. Employment was often obtained through the hiring fairs, when he would stand with his crook denoting his work, hoping to attract a new employer. The decline of hiring fairs from the late nineteenth century onwards meant that shepherds were hired by recommendation or through press advertisements,

Delicate clipping and combing as Shepherd Linkhorn, a shepherd of fifty years' experience, prepares a Southdown ram for showing at the Sussex County Show in 1947. The neck yoke and tether keep the animal still.

primarily the local newspaper, although some employers in the twentieth century did use the national farming press.

The shepherd earned more than most workers on the farm. In cash terms, his rate of pay was generally 2s a week more than the ordinary farm labourer's. The 17s a week which this might mean for a shepherd of the Yorkshire hills in the late nineteenth century were still far from high wages. The shepherd did receive some generous additional allowances, most notably his home, which was one of the best cottages on the farm, as befitted his status, and an allotment big enough for a cow or pigs. On the other hand, the terms of his annual hiring meant that extra piecework earnings at peak times, such as harvest, were not open to him, although there were some exceptions.

A shepherd with Herdwick rams near Coniston in the Lake District, January 1952.

He could receive a penny for each lamb reared (6d for twins), and 12–13s for every one hundred sheep sheared. He worked all the hours required, and they could be long. Lambing time brought him to as near 24-hour days as he could make it.

The status of the shepherd was recognized by the nineteenth-century census returns, which gave him an entry in the occupational returns separate from the other agricultural workers. There were 19,075 of them in the 1851 census of England and Wales, and numbers were rising slightly during the following decades to about 25,000. Even so, there were remarkably few when one remembers that there were then more than 200,000 farms, and the near-universality of sheep. Some shepherds probably escaped being returned as such, but equally, the work of keeping sheep was undertaken by people who were not always formally styled 'shepherd'. Under some farming regimes the sheep required relatively little attention, so that other workers could handle the flock, especially if it was not too large. The farmer himself might be his own shepherd, working with the assistance only of his sons and other family members. Pressure to keep down labour costs in the twentieth century helped make this a more common arrangement. Even those employed as shepherds were often required to undertake other tasks. An advertisement for a shepherd in Cambridgeshire in 1928 wanted him to be a hedger and ditcher as well. It is the same today, of course. The shepherd came into his own on larger farms which had sheep as one of the main lines.

Shepherds were almost all men. Little Bo Peep and the various depictions in folk song and bucolic paintings notwithstanding, it was not usual to find a shepherdess. The women who did get involved with tending the sheep were usually the wives and daughters of shepherds, helping out or deputizing at busy times. W. H. Hudson wrote of meeting a teenage girl in charge of a Sussex flock while the shepherd was elsewhere and all the other workers on the farm were busy with the harvest, but this, he noted, was a rare occurrence. The Second World War, which brought thousands of Land Girls to British farms, made little difference: the Land Girls were not often employed with the sheep. Since then things have changed. Any sense that shepherding skills were a male preserve has gone, and women have entered the sheepfold. The pressures of farming with fewer workers have been among the causes. It has become not uncommon for couples to work in partnership managing the sheep, but there are many lone shepherdesses as well. Shepherdesses are still in the minority, but there are probably more in the twenty-first century than at any other time.

Reading some of the literature gives the impression that shepherds were almost born to the job, and there certainly were many families in which there seemed to be a natural progression between generations. Son followed father, nephew followed uncle. One Sussex man recorded in 1850

Ida Rance was the shepherdess on her family's farm at Wendover, Buckinghamshire, in the late 1940s.

could trace his line back two hundred years, all working as shepherds. Caleb Bawcombe, one of the principal characters in W. H. Hudson's *A Shepherd's Life*, started working with sheep in childhood, working with his father, even being put in charge of the flock as young as six. Peter Gurney (C. S. Smith) wrote of Walter Griffin, of Alton Priors, Wiltshire, whose father and grandfather had been shepherds, as had various uncles.

However, this was far from universal. Michael Blann was born at Beeding, Sussex, in 1843, and lived to the age of 90. His father was not a shepherd, but Michael was sent out to work with sheep at nine years old and stayed with it. Many shepherds moved into the job from other work on the farm after, perhaps, a number of years spent as a general labourer. The farm labourer drafted in to help with the sheep at busy times, such as lambing, dipping and shearing, gradually gained knowledge and skill until he was able to find work as a shepherd in his own right. A few moved in from outside farming altogether. Walter Johnson, writing in 1925, mentioned a man who had left work in London for the Sussex countryside, where he ended up as a shepherd. Training was on the job, exclusively so until the twentieth century. Then agricultural colleges began to run courses on shepherding skills, teaching young farm workers and farmers how to handle sheep and dogs. Most of those who work with sheep now undergo some training of that nature.

The young lad without father's footsteps to follow could start as an apprentice shepherd. Shepherd lads, or farm lads, they were usually called; or they might be 'shepherd's boys', or 'shepherd's pages': the terms varied from district to district. Whatever the name, they could take on the role soon after leaving school. Their work depended on the size of the farm and its flock: they could be more or less full-time trainee shepherds where flocks were large; elsewhere they might be needed only at peak times. In Sussex there was an intermediate stage known as 'teg boy', after which the young man might progress to under shepherd and finally head shepherd.

At the other end of the career cycle, the shepherd could become a farm bailiff, or, like Gabriel Oak in Thomas Hardy's *Far From the Madding Crowd*, gain enough capital to become an independent flockmaster or farmer. Such farmer-shepherds were not uncommon amongst small farming communities in the south west. This could lead to some confusing nomenclature, with men such as Frank Whatley, shown in the photograph on page 6, addressed interchangeably as 'Farmer' or 'Shepherd'. But, as modern writers such as David Kennard testify, whether employed or farmers on their own account, a shepherd will always be a shepherd.

The shepherds who featured in literature were often those who had a long career. Rider Haggard in 1902 described George Shepherd, still working on the Downs above Andover aged over seventy, having started as a shepherd boy sixty years before. 'There he stood in the cold wind upon the bleak Down crest,' wrote Rider Haggard, 'watching the flock much as a dog does, and now and again passing the hurdles to do some little service to his flock ...'. Barclay Wills, who wrote about shepherds he encountered in Sussex in the

Young shepherds and farmers attending a course in shepherding at Shropshire Adult College in February 1953.

Shepherd's lad Robert Churly assists his shepherd John Barnes in weighing lambs for the Christmas market at Bradstock, Devon, in December 1961.

Opposite:
'An old shepherd', and his wife, photographed at the door of their Berkshire cottage in about 1890.

early twentieth century, described Walter Wooler of Pyecombe. He had been working for fifty-eight years when Wills met him. He had been born in 1856 in Alfriston, a village on the South Downs a few miles north east of Eastbourne. He was the son of a shepherd who moved to a new job at Pyecombe, another downland village about twenty miles away, when Walter was three months old. He followed in his father's footsteps, having charge of his first flock of five hundred ewes at the early age of sixteen. Wooler spent almost all his working life in Pyecombe; he returned to Alfriston to marry, but within a short while was back in Pyecombe where he stayed.

Such long careers were not uncommon. The fitness needed for a life in the open and for handling livestock kept the men active. And, despite the long hours, work in all weathers and recalcitrant sheep, shepherds generally loved their work. Oral history and the pen portraits of shepherds by such writers as W. H. Hudson all reveal men who revelled in the countryside, their sheep and their dogs. They were unwilling to give it up.

SHEPHERDING IN THE UPLANDS

T HE SKILLS of the shepherd were universal. His knowledge of the sheep, its habits and its ailments, his ability to control the flock, using the herding skills of sheep dogs – all these were common features. But the life of the upland shepherd was quite different from that of his counterpart on the southern Downs.

The upland shepherd was a man of the wide-open spaces. He looked after hardy breeds of sheep – the Cheviots, Welsh Mountain, Herdwick, Whiteface Dartmoor, and similar types that could stand the rigours of life at 500 feet or more above sea level. Much of the hill sheep farming of the eighteenth and nineteenth centuries was based on a breeding flock. Part of the flock was over-wintered on the hills – the sheep were hardy enough – but numbers were limited by availability of winter feed. Most of the season's lambs were brought down to lowland pastures where they were brought on for the fatstock market. Some hill farmers had their own lowland pastures, but most sold their lambs in the autumn to graziers on the lowlands.

Although the shepherd spent most of his time out on the upland pastures, there were occasions when he had to gather the flock and bring it downhill to the farmstead. Preparation for tupping was one, lambing and weaning, and clipping were others; and there could be other occasions when all or part of the flock needed to be brought together for an injection or other treatment. It was not always a simple matter and two or three days could be occupied in bringing a flock down from the hills.

The hill flocks roamed widely across the rough pastures. Each flock, though, had its own grazing ground on the fells; the boundaries were not, of course, marked. On the fell farms of Lakeland, the new farmer took on the flock of sheep with his tenancy, and passed on a flock of equal value to the next tenant when he left. The shepherds could spend weeks with them away from home. The weather could be inclement; there were often shelters for the shepherd and the sheep. In the Scottish border country the shelter was known as a hirsel. In the summer, however, shepherds would often sleep out, bedding down in the heather. It could be lonely as well, although the

Opposite:
Two men drive
their flock of
Swaledale sheep
down from
grazing in the
Durham fells,
September 1959.

Winter feeding
in Perthshire:
shepherd David
Ogilvie brings
hay to his flock,
February 1953.

Mist swirls down
the northern
Welsh mountains
as shepherds
go out with
their flock.

The flock in the hills, an early-twentieth-century picture postcard.

shepherds compensated for that in their gatherings at markets, fairs, sheepdog trials and shows. The fell shepherds of Cumberland would gather once a year over sheep shearing.

There was another meeting in the autumn – the 'shepherds' meet'. This was when the shepherds came together to exchange lost sheep. Although their flock management exploited the sheep's ability to learn its surroundings

This rescue party of men and dogs has successfully found one buried sheep on the hills of Sutherland in February 1978.

and its usual routes – what in the Lake District is termed 'hefting' – inevitably some sheep went missing. They were usually picked up by neighbouring shepherds, who kept them with their own flocks until, once a year, the grand exchange took place. The older, more experienced shepherds led proceedings, often able to recognize sheep from different flocks even if their markings had faded. To help identification, shepherds and farmers had their *Shepherds' Guide*, a book which reproduced all the marks allocated to every farmer of the locality, and listed the dates of the meets. The first guide was published in 1817 by Joseph Walker of Ullswater. Several editions of these guides followed, and in later years publication was mainly through the various

Sometimes horseback was the best means of rounding up sheep on the hills: a scene on Exmoor in the 1950s.

The shepherds' meet at Mardale, near Bampton, Cumbria, in November 1958. The men are gathering round to identify the strays.

local associations of fell farmers. A *Shepherds' Guide* was still being published in 2000.

The meets were held all over the upland areas: there were at least half a dozen in Lakeland. The magazine *The Globe* reported on the autumn gathering of Yorkshire shepherds on 7 November 1878, when 121 sheep were returned

Right: Some of
the sheep marks
used by farmers in
Cumberland, from
Gate's *Shepherds'
Guide* published
in 1879.

Below: Filling the
feeding troughs for
a flock of Masham
sheep (a Blackface
and Wensleydale
cross) on the
north Lincolnshire
hills at Appleby
in March 1935.

to their rightful owners. After
the business was conducted, the
meeting settled into a social affair.
The local hunt might gather;
there could be sheepdog trials.
There was certainly a hearty meal
in the inn, followed by an evening
of conversation, story-telling and
singing. The meets continued in
many places at least until the foot
and mouth outbreak of 2001
decimated many upland flocks.
It was difficult to get the
tradition going again, but a few
continue, albeit with a smaller
exchange function.

THE LOWLAND SHEPHERD

Arthur Young in the 1760s described Salisbury Plain as being 'inhabited by only a few shepherds and their flocks.' At that time the lowland shepherd, in common with his counterpart in the hills, used to have wide areas of land to graze. They were known as sheep walks, pastures covering extensive tracts of such areas as the Downs, the Wolds and Romney Marsh. But his life became more enclosed as the farmers tried to increase productivity by growing more arable crops and better-quality pasture. The sheep walks of the chalk Downs and Wolds and the limestone of the Cotswolds were turned into fields growing cereals for the market and turnips for the sheep to eat. This process, which went on during the nineteenth century, greatly reduced the extent of the natural grassland, so that by the 1870s most had gone. There were still some areas of more open downland in Wiltshire, for example.

The shepherd and his flock were now confined to the fields – which, even so, were still large by most standards. But, instead of taking the flock freely across pasture, he was now engaged in closer management as farming became more intensive. It was a form of farming that required greater input of labour, and much of the increase in numbers of shepherds between the 1850s and 1870s can be attributed to the 'sheep-corn' husbandry of lowland England.

The former sheep pastures had been turned into fields growing a succession of cereal and fodder crops. Of these, the root crop of turnips or swede was of prime importance. Rather than lift the roots, it was common to bring the sheep into the fields between autumn and spring to

A Berkshire shepherd stands by the hurdle gate to the sheep enclosure, with his Border Collie sheepdog at his feet.

A postcard published in the early twentieth century showing a sheepfold on the Wiltshire downland below Westbury white horse.

WESTBURY WHITE HORSE

Springtime harrowing stops while the sheep are led by on their way to finish a field of turnips during the 1930s at Kiddington, Oxfordshire

eat the crop in situ, a system known as folding. Other crops were grown for the same purpose, including carrots, cabbage and kale. The shepherd had to ensure that the sheep progressed across the field of turnips in orderly fashion, leaving an even distribution of manure for the following crop of cereals,

Carrying gate
hurdles out
to the field.

Hampshire
Down ram
lambs in a field
of trefoil clover,
enclosed with
wattle hurdles.
Extra feed is
being poured
into the troughs.
Buckinghamshire
in the 1930s.

by setting up folds within the fields. Temporary fences marked off the folds. Most often these fences were constructed from hurdles made of hazel or wood; sometimes wire netting was used. The shepherd had to move the fences into position. The hazel hurdles were twigs woven round a frame into wattle, and they were light, easy to move and fix in the ground. The shepherd could do the work on his own most of the time. The wooden hurdles were known as gate hurdles, made of willow in a similar pattern to a farm gate, but far less substantial. They were a little heavier than the wattle hurdles, and might require two pairs of hands in setting them up.

These hurdles were used for other temporary shelters, to protect ewes and young lambs, as stockades to corral the sheep before dipping, and for other needs. There was enough demand to provide a good living for the hurdlemakers, who specialised in either the wattle or gate hurdles. Managing the sheep in the fold of roots was only a part of the lowland shepherd's work. There were fields of pasture as well, to which the shepherd carried supplies of additional food – oilcake, corn and chopped roots all fed from troughs. Maintaining a supply of water was also important, for many of the fields on chalk downlands were dry. As well as these jobs, the shepherd managed the lambing and weaning of lambs in spring, shearing and dipping in early summer and the tupping in autumn. He had to maintain the quality of the flock, attending to veterinary care, keeping the sheep's feet clean and sound, its body clean, and seeing that wethers reached peak condition in time for market. All in all, this turned the shepherd into a very skilled worker with greater responsibility, only partly reflected in his wage.

Opposite top: Unloading feed for Kerry sheep from a tractor-drawn trailer on Mr Wilcox's farm at Aldworth, Gloucestershire, February 1959.

Opposite Bottom: The water cart was an essential part of many a sheep farm's equipment. Here the carts are in use on the Berkshire Downs in the 1930s.

Below: Shepherds prepared much of the feed for their flock themselves. This hand-held chopper for preparing roots was one of their tools.

Bottom: To feed sheep and lambs in the fields troughs and racks of various sorts were used, from the improvised home-made wooden construction to patent designs supplied by manufacturers. This one, which combined a rack for hay and trough for roots or water, was one of several made by Reeves of Bratton, Wiltshire. It was 10 feet long, intended to feed 20–24 sheep at once.

COMBINED SHEEP RACK AND TROUGH.

R & J. REEVES & SON BRATTON

THE WORK OF THE SHEPHERD

THE SHEPHERD'S ROLE was to look after the sheep, and to look over the sheep, watching out for their needs. In Romney Marsh shepherds were traditionally known as 'lookers'. The term was also found in neighbouring districts of Sussex and Essex, applied variously to those who looked after sheep and cattle.

The life of the shepherd and sheep farmer was punctuated by a number of regular events throughout the year: lambing, shearing, fairs and so on. The cycle began with tupping, putting the ram to the ewe. The time for tupping varied according to district and the time for lambing. The ewe's gestation period is a very precise twenty-one weeks, which meant that tupping could be arranged for the fall of lambs to be when the farming needed them. The availability of spring grass to feed the ewes and lambs used to be important in the calculation of times, but the greater use of turnips and feed bought in during the nineteenth century gave the farmer and shepherd more flexibility. They could not be entirely independent of seasons and climate, however, and regional patterns remained. On lowland farms the ram was introduced early in autumn for the first lambs to drop in late winter and early spring. The hill farmer delayed tupping, sometimes as late as December. This provided lambs in the period from January to May. There was one exception: the Dorset Horn breed can produce two drops of lambs a year, with a second in October. Whatever the timing, the ram's work was spread over a period of three to four weeks, to give a similar spread in the lambing season. Having spent the rest of the year in relative idleness, the ram had to be brought into condition before he was introduced to the ewes, so the shepherd had to give him some exercise, even taking him for walks like a dog.

Lambing was – and is – the most crucial time of year for the shepherd. So much depended on a successful lambing, both in terms of the potential income from the flock, and its contribution to other aspects of mixed farming. Preparations for lambing time were made in the weeks beforehand. Sheep being fundamentally hardy animals, there was a strong preference for lambs

Opposite:
Dipping pedigree
Hampshire Down
lambs at Shapwick,
Dorset, in the
1970s, with
policemen in
attendance to
see that all is
done correctly.

When this photograph was taken in the 1960s, triplet lambs were less common than they have since become. The head shepherd gently holds three less than a day old.

to be born in the fields, even in such exposed parts of the country as Romney Marsh. The sheep were not simply left out in the fields to get on with lambing: 'maternity wards' were prepared. These might be no more than a field set aside, with feed available for ewes and their lambs, and some temporary folds for those animals requiring special attention. This could be the pattern on upland farms with the hardiest breeds of sheep. More elaborate lambing folds were constructed elsewhere, especially on southern lowland farms. These folds were constructed with walls of close-woven hurdles lined and roofed with straw to mitigate the effects of the cold and wind. With insatiable appetite, the shepherd scoured the farm for straw for the outside walls, and bedding. Inside the fold, more hurdles were used to separate the individual pens. It was laborious manual work getting the hurdles and thatch arranged. To build a temporary lambing pen now, the shepherd uses a tractor and big round bales, which create a very effective walled shelter.

The alternative to the lambing fold made of hurdles in the field was a permanent pen in the farmstead, often in or near the stackyard, to which the ewes were brought from the fields. It was not a popular arrangement with flockmasters and shepherds, who argued that the distance from the sheep's

Tom Gloyn, the shepherd at Shapwick, Dorset, trims one of his rams, smartening him up before sending him on hire for tupping neighbouring flocks.

feed was too great. On lowland farms there were some who were using sheds by the 1930s, and since the 1950s there has been a turnaround. Lambing sheds have become common on lowland and upland farms alike, and are now the usual arrangement. The sheds are arranged with series of lambing pens,

A Kentish-style shelter for young lambs at New Romney, March 1936.

Inside the sturdy lambing shelters on a farm near Kingham, Oxfordshire, a tiny new-born lamb is fed from a bottle, February 1952.

from which the ewes and their lambs are moved to individual pens where they can become established before being turned out into the fields.

W. J. Malden, in a textbook written before 1914, advised that 'the shepherd should not be given any other work to do during the busiest season of lambing'. He must have experienced farmers placing unreasonable demands on their shepherds when they were the ones needing assistance. The ewes and lambs

Some of the ewes and their lambs have been brought outside the wattle-and-straw lambing pens on Mr Lanley's farm near Taunton in February 1955. Shepherd and dog keep watch, while parked nearby are a water cart and mobile shepherd's hut.

It is open day on the farm, when the public are welcomed inside the big, airy lambing shed. The young shepherd is on hand to tend to lambing ewes and talk to the visitors.

needed continual attention, ensuring that mothers were accepting their lambs, feeding, changing the litter in the pens. Assistance here was invaluable, while on a large farm someone else was generally required to attend to the non-breeding part of the flock. The shepherd paid close attention to the new lambs during their first few weeks to ensure they settled in the fields. After about twelve weeks it was usual to dock the lambs' tails as a precaution against disease.

A ewe which loses its lamb is usually turned into a foster mother either for an orphan or to take a lamb from a ewe that has two, or nowadays, three lambs. To help the ewe accept the alien infant, the lamb is clothed with the skin from her dead offspring. The shepherd is putting the dead lamb's skin on the one to be adopted in this scene from the 1930s.

The lambs have to be accounted for almost as soon as they are born, with ownership marks and numbers applied to them, as this photograph from the 1930s demonstrates.

After being with their mothers through most of the summer, the lambs were separated from the ewes, an operation in process on a Cumberland farm in 1943.

The timing for summer shearing of the fleece was critical: too early and the shorn sheep might suffer from a cold snap, too late and they were inconvenienced by the old fleece dropping off while the new one grew underneath. The correct time for shearing was generally from June to early July in lowland areas, July in the hills.

Before shearing it was common to wash the sheep to get the grease out of the fleece. It was not essential, but the price for unwashed wool was considerably lower than washed – so most farmers did it. Running water was preferred, so if there was a stream with sufficient depth and flow it would be used for the sheep wash. Long tradition established such places on the map, with names such as Sheepwash. Where there was no stream a washing pit would have to be constructed – on Romney Marsh they called it a 'sheep tun'. Washing was not popular either with sheep, shepherds or the additional hands brought in to help. The sheep had to be rounded up and brought to the washing. Once there, there was much jostling, as sheep tried to avoid getting wet, which in the process could end up with men being dragged into the stream. Pressure on farm labour and declining returns from wool meant that washing became less common after the Second World War. The introduction of mechanized washing in wool-processing factories in the 1960s finally killed off farm washing.

Sheep shearing is a skill requiring stamina to hold sheep that would prefer to be elsewhere, while manipulating them to cut the fleece first round the neck, then the body, and finally the hindquarters. There were specialist sheep shearers who toured from farm to farm clipping the fleece. Some were from Australia and New Zealand, spending the antipodean winter in Britain. Often very competitive, keen to demonstrate their skill and speed with the clippers, some of these men achieved some renown. They entered shearing contests, which started on a regular footing in about 1815. Not every farm employed the visiting shearers. On many it was the shepherd, with perhaps some additional help, who undertook the shearing. Even if the specialist shearers were brought in, the shepherd had a busy few weeks, for he was on hand to

Washing the sheep in a river, although at the moment the photograph was taken, the men were up to their waists in water, while the sheep were keeping dry. Meanwhile, the operation provided some entertainment for the onlookers in this scene set for an Edwardian picture postcard.

35

catch the sheep, and do a health check on them as they came away from the shearing. He would call on additional help for catching and tethering sheep, marking the sheep after they had been shorn, tallying the number of sheep, and bagging and weighing the fleeces. Clipping could be a social and communal affair: on the hill farms of the north neighbouring farms would work together, pooling their labour, to shear each other's sheep, and a timetable would be organized for the shearing on each farm. After the day's work an evening together of dining, singing and dancing followed. On a grander scale, some landowners, such as the Duke of Bedford, made their estate sheep shearing into an occasion for showing off their improved breeds of stock in the early nineteenth century.

The introduction of powered clippers reduced that interdependence. Using them a sheep could be sheared in a minute or so, compared with five taken by a skilled shearer with hand clippers. Sheep had been shorn by hand until the late eighteenth century using large scissors made by the blacksmith. Industrial techniques introduced a new material, spring steel, which allowed the creation of a new design for sheep shears with triangular blades. Mechanical clippers were introduced in the late nineteenth century. Frank Wolseley was granted the first patent for a sheep-shearing machine

A single sheep
being shorn
at Mytton,
near Clitheroe,
Lancashire, c. 1900.

in 1877 in Australia. A British firm was established a few years later, the Wolseley Sheep Shearing Machine Company, and was one of the two that dominated the market for this equipment. Herbert Austin was the manager of the business, and from this connection arose the associated Wolseley motor company.

The first mechanical clippers were powered by horse engine or by hand. Hand-operated shears required an assistant to crank the handle to generate power. They remained in use for a long time – Wolseleys were still

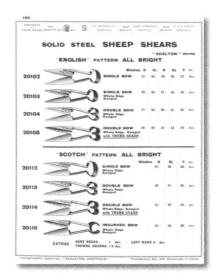

The familiar pattern of sheep shears is primarily a product of industrialisation, developed in the eighteenth century. The loop of spring steel links two triangular blades. After squeezing the clippers together for the cut, they spring quickly back open. There were many varieties of the basic pattern, with different styles of blade and bow, as this selection from the 1915 catalogue of C. T. Skelton & Co. Ltd, of Sheffield, shows.

making them in the 1960s. By that time other sources of power were more often employed, certainly for large flocks. The portable oil engine was the first alternative to hand power, but as electricity reached the farms it came into common use. Powered clippers did not immediately displace the specialist shearers, but farmers did find that shepherds or other men on the farm –

themselves included – could gain sufficient skill to handle the work. The need for elaborate communal arrangements between farms declined, and shepherds were left to deal with their own flock, with a modest amount of additional labour brought in.

There were medieval laws requiring flockmasters to have their sheep marked to denote ownership. Diggery Venn in Thomas Hardy's *The Return of the Native* was a raddle (or reddle, or ruddle) man, who supplied the red dye, a mixture of red ochre and size, used to mark the fleece. Dyes could fade and be clipped off at shearing, and the more

Listers, of Dursley in Gloucestershire, were the main rivals of the Wolseley Sheep Shearing Co. This is one of their hand-powered shearing machines advertised in their catalogue for 1915.

Three branding
irons for putting
owners' marks
on sheep.

One man shears
while the other
marks the Exmoor
Horn sheep on
a farm in north
Devon in
the 1960s.

permanent mark of a nick clipped in the ear, made when the animals are lambs, has been used since at least the fifteenth century. Each owner had his own shape of clip; in many places these were assigned to the farm, not the farmer, and were thus transferred to each new tenant. More recent times have seen the use of plastic ear tags to record the sheep's ownership and the data required by government. Horned sheep might have a brand mark on the horn, and more generally brand marks were stamped on the body after shearing using pitch or graphite, later superseded by proprietary marking fluids.

Left: The red paint used to mark sheep came to be supplied by industrial manufacturers, who sold it in sticks like this one.

Below: An ear punch used in Gloucestershire in the nineteenth century.

Sheep are prone to a number of ailments and diseases, and the shepherd had to be prepared to deal with most of them himself. The nineteenth-century shepherd inherited some simple, ancient remedies, such as wrapping the bark of a birch round a broken leg to form a cast, birch bark having antiseptic properties. By the century's end proprietorial lotions and potions were more usual. The shepherd's basic stock of equipment for treatment and hygiene recommended in late-nineteenth-century textbooks included disinfectants (Jeyes' fluid), carbolic soap, 'penny sponges' and a metal pail for washing his hands. Dressings, medicines and surgical tools were also part of his stock. Medicines administered as liquids were known as drenches, and the cup from which these were poured down the sheep's throat was a drenching horn. An indispensable tool was his knife used for trimming hoofs and horns, cutting string and a host of other little tasks.

One disease common in sheep was scab caused by parasitic ticks and lice. For centuries flockmasters sought to counteract the ticks by applying a salve

Drenching horns were made of a cow's horn with the core removed, and the end shaped into a lip to enable the medicine to be poured down the sheep's throat.

A single-bladed folding knife used by shepherds for basic veterinary work, cutting twine and other needs. This one has Cooper's dip branding.

to the fleece. Some medieval references mention the use of oil and tallow. By the late eighteenth century various treatments were used. A mixture of tar and butter was one, while tobacco juice, turpentine, mercury and other more or less efficacious products were also used. Whatever it was made from, applying the salve was labour-intensive work, requiring the sheep to be strapped up on a bench while the salve was worked in by hand. No more than ten sheep a day could be treated in this fashion according to *The General View of the Agriculture of the North Riding of Yorkshire* published in 1800. The autumn, about the time of tupping, was when the salve was most often applied, with another application in spring. A salve box was one of the essential items of shepherding equipment; they were usually of modest size, easily carried, and resulting in little loss of salve if they were knocked over.

This photograph dated 1890 shows sheep being salved by hand on a farm at Hesket, in Cumberland. A group of lads has been recruited for the task.

In the 1830s William Cooper began selling a mixture of arsenic and sulphur as a treatment for scab, and this could be applied in dilute form. The business he founded became one of the biggest manufacturers of sheep dip, for dipping the sheep in a bath of the liquid chemicals was soon established as the best application of Cooper's compound. Dipping was soon common practice, but was not universal until it was made compulsory in 1907, from which time a policeman had to be in attendance to verify that the whole flock had been dipped correctly. Dipping was even less popular a task than washing the sheep. Plenty of men were needed to chase recalcitrant sheep and ensure that they went through the bath. Sheep had to be completely submerged, and to achieve that the men used

How a salve box was worn on the shepherd's arm, a demonstration from a museum collection.

A poster advertising Cooper's sheep dip, printed in the 1900s.

COOPER'S DIP FOR YOUR FLOCK

MR. LINCOLN TO MR. CHEMIST :—
"DIP PLEASE, AND IT MUST BE COOPER'S"

A sheep dipping hook.

Thomas Bigg's portable sheep dip of the mid-nineteenth century. There were other versions which, instead of swinging the sheep across in a basket, had the animals as it were walking the plank to arrive in the dipping trough. Modern portable dips follow roughly the same principle.

long-handled dipping hooks to push the animals under. The men were in danger of being soaked with the noxious dips. Concern over the safety and environmental impact of dipping chemicals grew during the second half of the twentieth century, especially after organo-phosphate dips became common. Concerns about the safety of men and sheep led to the removal of compulsion to dip in 1991. Instead a general requirement was imposed upon farmers to ensure that they treated scab effectively.

The mid-nineteenth century censuses recorded men who were described as sheep dippers. Some of them were employed taking portable sheep dips round the farms. These were big baths on wheels with a ramp on each end for the sheep to enter and leave. There were few of these specialist sheep dippers, as most farmers preferred to use their own men and build a permanent dip, a pit of brick, stone or concrete with holding pens and stockades to lead the sheep in and out. Once compulsion and inspection were instituted, such structures became more necessary. The wheel has turned again recently, for ever more stringent rules about the application of the chemicals have led to the return of the specialist sheep-dipper taking his mobile dipping baths on contract hire round the farms.

Improved Moveable Dipping Apparatus.

The points worthy of especial notice are the saving of labour, there being only three men required, (besides the shepherd, to catch and get ready the sheep), instead of five, as with the ordinary dipping apparatus. Price in London, £14.

Sheep going
to Shrewsbury
market by
horse-drawn
wagon, January
1939.

The sales of lambs and sheep provided further occasions for the shepherd to leave his fields. Before the sale he had the job of sorting the sheep ready for market, and then he would often attend the fair along with his master. He might take the sheep to the market himself, but they were often entrusted to specialist drovers. Distance played a great part in this decision: the shepherd was more likely to take sheep to local sales.

One of the subjects discussed in the late-nineteenth-century literature on shepherds was whether British shepherds led their flocks or drove them from behind. The biblical passage in which Jesus says he is the good shepherd, leading his sheep, caused writers to wonder whether that was a purely Palestinian trait. The answer was that British shepherds did both lead and drive their sheep, as appropriate, whether across the fields or along the road.

Driving sheep along the road, except between fields, was superseded by motor transport. There had been horse-drawn sheep wagons and carts, but their capacity was limited; they were useful for small flocks and the prize stock. Motor lorries, with their double-deck bodies, could carry far more and by the end of the 1920s took away the necessity for the shepherd to drive sheep to market.

From mid-summer onwards there was a succession of fairs and markets, which grew in number and scale during the nineteenth century as sheep farming expanded. Bellingham in Northumberland was one of many places where new sales were established in the mid-nineteenth century. Some of the fairs were immense. Weyhill, outside Andover, was perhaps the greatest. According to Daniel Defoe, Weyhill Michaelmas fair handled 500,000 sheep in the eighteenth century, but the 200,000 quoted in reports in the mid-nineteenth century were probably more accurate. East Ilsley, on the Berkshire Downs, was another place to attract buyers and sellers from a wide area to its markets and fairs for sheep. 'At first sight it really appears to consist almost entirely of public-houses,' L. Salmon wrote of Ilsley in 1909. They catered for the shepherds, drovers, farmers and dealers who came for the markets and fairs held fortnightly from Easter to July and again in August and September. The distances travelled by buyers and sellers, and the early start to the morning's sale, meant that many stayed overnight at the inns.

By the 1930s many of the fairs had closed, having been replaced by fatstock markets and auction marts. The sales established at Bellingham in the 1860s survive as auctions, and still handle large numbers of stock, and they can still draw the shepherds in to observe the action. Going to a fair often meant a night or two away, another occasion for shepherds to get together, resulting in tales of some less-than-steady homeward journeys. The advent of motor transport compressed the visit to markets usually to no more than a day, but there could still be some time for the tap room.

Another feature of the shepherd's autumn calendar was the show. There were dozens of local shows started during the nineteenth century.

Sheep being loaded onto the motor van that took away the need for the shepherd to drive his flock to market.

The shepherds from the country around drove their sheep to the show, where, amid fierce rivalry, they would compete for the championship. It was, of course, another chance for shepherds to socialize, with other competitions and entertainments, from cake-baking to tug-of-war, going on around.

Outside the busy times, such as lambing, shepherds' lives could take on a more leisurely aspect, giving them plenty of time for 'studying their sheep', as A. G. Street described it. They managed to study other things as well, and many shepherds were well-read, self-taught men. James Hogg became well known as a poet, and there were others who were well-versed in the Bible. There were many musicians amongst the shepherds. Michael Blann in Sussex was a collector and performer of the folk music of the Downs, which he played on the flute and penny whistle.

Alresford sheep fair in the 1930s, attracting interested onlookers as well as farmers and shepherds. Two of the lorries that were beginning to supplant the drover are in the background.

SHEPHERDS
AND THEIR DOGS

IN THE 1790s William Marshall remarked on the skill with which shepherds in west Devon handled sheep with their dogs. With these dogs in control there was hardly any need to pen sheep. If sheep needed to be inspected, the shepherd sent the dog to herd them into a corner of the field where they remained, guarded by the dog, while the shepherd or farmer did his work. All the shepherd had to do, Marshall wrote, clearly impressed, was whistle or shout, and the dog responded and flew off to the sheep. 'The stragglers are driven in, by the circuitous route of the dogs, which keep flying round, from side to side, until the flock be gathered round the shepherd.'

Marshall made it clear he was describing something that was far from usual practice, and indeed, the use of the dog in sheep management was changing. Dogs had been employed with sheep for centuries, but their primary role had been as guardians, to protect the flock from attack, in particular from wolves. The extinction of wolves in Britain reduced that need to guard the flock – the shepherd's concern in that regard has since become the protection of sheep from worrying by domestic dogs. Instead shepherds turned to exploit the herding abilities of dogs, but there were still many who were not sure about that at the end of the eighteenth century. The dog would injure the sheep, they objected.

By the middle of the nineteenth century the doubts had almost entirely been cast aside, and the value of a well-trained dog for herding the flock was appreciated. James Hogg (1770–1835), the 'Ettrick Shepherd', famed for his poetry as well as his shepherding, wrote that 'A single shepherd and his dog will accomplish more in gathering a stock of sheep from a Highland farm than twenty could do without dogs.'

Nearly every shepherd now employs a Border Collie as his sheepdog. It is the most popular breed in Britain, and in many other parts of the world. So universal has the Border Collie become that it is hard to imagine any other breed being used with sheep. That was far from the case in the past. The Old English Sheepdog was once common in the south of England. It used to be called the Sussex, and among its attributes was a greater tolerance of heat,

Opposite:
A shepherd in southern England in the 1930s–40s poses with his Border Collie dog. As well as his crook he is holding his pipe; in his shoulder bag he has some of the tools he needs for the day.

A dog
demonstrating
prowess in
rounding
the sheep.

being able to keep working during a summer day, when the Border Collie would want to rest under a tree. Welsh hill farmers had their Welsh Collie dogs while in northern Scotland the Bearded Collie used to be common. The intelligence of the Border Collie, and its controlling abilities, have combined to make this the most popular sheepdog in the twentieth century. Other breeds have become rare, or bred into show dogs, so that the Old English has largely lost its image as a working dog.

Two Old English
sheepdogs
with their flock
feeding, Burnham,
Buckinghamshire,
1930s.

A lamb encounters
a sheepdog,
Englefield,
Berkshire, 1930s.

A good dog is such an asset that shepherds and drovers have invested considerable effort into choosing the right one, or the most likely looking pup to train. Increased mobility resulted in shepherds travelling miles to attend

Wasdale Head
shepherds' meet,
held at the foot
of Great Gable,
in Cumberland in
October 1950.
The sheepdogs
were being judged
in this photo.

sales or visit breeders. Sales such as Sennybridge in south Wales and Skipton in Yorkshire have come to attract crowds in the thousands, by no means all shepherds and flock-owners. This tended further to accentuate the dominance of the Border Collie in Britain, with prices rising for good pedigree animals. The International Sheep Dog Society started recording the dogs' lineage in 1949, further assisting the search for quality.

Shepherds have usually had at least two sheepdogs, often three or four. They would want at least one skilled and experienced dog, and a younger dog or pup in training. Then they might have dogs with different skills, some being much better at rounding up sheep, others skilled at dealing with the individual animal in difficulty. The large number of dogs required meant that when an excise duty on dogs was introduced in 1796, to curb the number of strays in towns, shepherds were faced with large bills. Representations to the Chancellor from one of Northumberland's leading landowners and farmers secured the shepherd an exemption from the tax, but not until 1828.

Another of the skills required of the dog was to drive the sheep. Sheep had to be brought down from the hills to lowland pasture, and along the tracks and lanes to markets and sales. Two or three dogs to keep the flock moving and catch strays were invaluable. Shepherds used some of their regular dogs for this job, but the specialist drovers engaged in long-distance transport of livestock, before the railways captured this trade, looked for

Michael Tory leads his flock of Hampshire Downs through the village of Shapwick, Dorset, on the way to fresh pasture.

Intense concentration on the faces of men and dogs watching a sheepdog trial in Scotland in the 1950s.

dogs with special driving skills. Dogs with patience, who would not rush the sheep, were especially favoured. So important was skill in driving that breeders of the Welsh Collie gave the breed two sub-divisions – the field (or 'heading') dogs and the driving dogs. For droving, too, the Border Collie came to supplant other breeds: indeed, it is possibly the influence of the drovers that lay behind the spread of this breed throughout the sheep world.

The International Sheep Dog Society was founded in 1906 to promote better flock management through improvement to the dogs, because 'without good working dogs the job of the shepherd ... is well nigh impossible.' One of the things the society took under its wing was the

A competitor whistling his commands at the English National Sheepdog Trials in 1960.

sheepdog trials, and it continues to manage them to this day. Organized competitions grew out of informal meetings in the 1870s: the first major trials being at Bala, north Wales, in 1873. Shepherds from Wales competed with their fellows from Scotland, demonstrating the lengths to which they were already prepared to go to take part. The sheepdog trials provided another opportunity for shepherds to get together, in friendly rivalry over the skills of their dogs. The bigger meetings have also attracted wider interest, for a while aided by the success of the television programme *One Man and His Dog*.

THE SHEPHERD'S TOOLS AND EQUIPMENT

A FTER HIS DOG, the thing most associated with a shepherd is his crook, used both to catch sheep and as a walking stick. There were two basic types of crook: the neck crook with a hook wide enough to go round the neck of a sheep or, more particularly, a lamb, and the leg crook, of narrower neck to catch the animal by its foot. These were often called leg 'cleeks'. Within the two types, there was scope for many variations of design.

Crooks have usually been made from sticks of hazel or ash, but other woods were used, elderberry, for example. A length of 3 feet 6 inches to 5 feet was most common, but some southern shepherds used much longer shafts of 7 feet or more. The shepherd often selected the stick himself, and took it to a stick-maker (or stick dresser) to be shaped and have the curved head put on. A ram's horn, heated and moulded to shape, was favoured by many shepherds, especially in the north. The Dorset Horn sheep was reckoned by many to produce the best horn, but, despite the breed's name, most of these sheep were hornless (or 'polled'), making its horns hard to come by; horn from other breeds and other animals would have to be used. Metal heads were the alternative, and used almost exclusively on leg crooks. The heads were mostly made by the blacksmith. Second-hand metal, often from gun barrels, was a popular material for fashioning a crook. The shepherd often specified the shape he wanted, but some blacksmiths became known for their particular patterns. Barclay Wills commented on the crooks made in Pyecombe and Falmer in Sussex; other writings and museum collections refer to crooks as 'Pyecombe pattern', 'Kingston pattern' and so on. The shaft of the crook was often embellished with carvings – motifs, often of dogs, chosen by the shepherd to give an individual touch to his crook. Shepherds might learn the art of carving themselves, but they were as likely to turn to the experienced hands of the stick-dresser. The tradition of stick carving has been maintained by a mixture of professional and amateur practitioners. In the north country, the Border Stick Dressers Association, founded in 1951, brings together those who share the interest.

Lambing meant night work, and shepherds used their own style of lantern lit by a candle. They kept on with these long after hurricane lamps and oil lamps had become common, and in preference to electric torches and cycle lamps. Lantern light was subdued compared with the others, not so bright that it might upset the ewe. A candle was also less likely to cause much damage if the lantern was knocked over, whereas oil could quickly cause a fire if spilled on to the straw. The lanterns were usually made of brass, iron or tin, with conical top. The windows were of horn rather than glass; it was the

This shepherd, posing with his crook in the 1920s, is believed to be Shepherd Andrews of East Hendred, in Berkshire.

A selection of shepherds' crooks and sticks, of wood, horn and metal, in the Museum of English Rural Life.

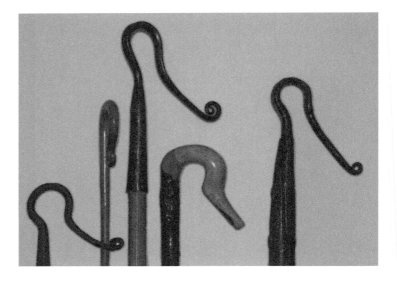

A ewe wearing a bell, with its lamb in a pen for young lambs on a downland farm in the 1930s.

traditional material, for centuries cheaper than glass. Even after glass became more readily available in the nineteenth century, many shepherds stuck with the horn lantern because it would not shatter if knocked, and it diffused the light. On most designs one window opened to allow access to the candle.

It was common until the early twentieth century, at least, to put a bell round the sheep's neck. The practice was more usual in southern England than in hill farming districts – one was more likely to hear the tinkling of flocks on the downlands than anywhere else. The bells gave an indication to the shepherd of where his sheep were, and could warn him of dangers or intruders. Yet, while such usefulness was undoubtedly true, Barclay Wills, Peter Gurney and others have commented on the fact that shepherds simply enjoyed the sound, and company, of the bells. One of the shepherds W. H. Hudson spoke to said, 'It is lonesome with the flock on the downs. ... The bells keep us from feeling it too much.' The fact that they were as much for ornament as use perhaps accounts for the rapid decline in the practice of equipping sheep with bells from the mid-twentieth century onwards under pressure from changing farming methods, although some flockmasters have maintained the tradition down to recent times.

Not all the sheep in the flock wore bells. One shepherd told Hudson he had 'Just forty, and I wish there were eighty' bells in his flock. But the shepherds had to buy the bells out of their own pockets, which were not deep enough to afford more than perhaps a couple of dozen. That pleased the neighbours, who did not always find the noise of bells as comforting as the shepherd did. People would complain about the loudness of particularly large bells on sheep driven through villages, even where the residents were used to stock passing through. The sheep to receive the bells, attached with a leather collar, were carefully selected – the more adventurous, who would lead the flock, or the more timid, perhaps in more danger of getting lost. The bells themselves were made of sheet metal hammered to shape by local smiths, or they were cast from brass or copper by foundries. Cast bells were more expensive; local foundries in the southern sheep-farming counties made many, but firms in the Midlands also cast them, selling some to overseas markets. The bells were made in a number of different shapes, the most

Following pages: Arthur Rush, a shepherd in Essex, with his ewes and lambs by the night-light of his lantern (and a healthy dose of the photographer's lighting), c. 1950.

The principal types of sheep bell. On the left is a canister type, next a clucket bell, the most common. The two on the right are cast bells, one similar to a hand bell, and with a tone to match, and one a brass 'cup' bell.

A Shepherd's hut made by Reeves of Bratton, Wiltshire, from their early-twentieth-century catalogues.

By 1955 the shepherd had some mod cons in his hut – television and electric light. Shepherd Walter Jacklin worked on Cliff Farm, Hackthorn, Lincolnshire.

common types being the canister, the cup, and the clucket bell. They varied in size and tone, from light tinkle to sonorous clonk.

Thomas Hardy's Gabriel Oak was to be found one night playing his flute in his shepherd's hut. This hut was a portable caravan that provided semi-permanent shelter for the shepherd. It was associated mainly with the lowland areas, especially the Downs. Shepherds had always needed shelters for themselves and their sheep, and in earlier centuries they had created them out of bushes, usually hawthorn. The trees were grown and shaped in such a fashion as to provide a hollow into which the shepherd, with a bed of straw, could find shelter. This was the 'shepherd's bush', recalled now in the name of a district of west London. Another form of shelter was a miniature cave hollowed out of a bank, confusingly also called a shepherd's hut in some quarters. The 'lookers' of Romney Marsh often had purpose-built brick shelters, which provided better accommodation; most have disappeared now.

A caravan was also an improvement on the shelter of trees, and, as sheep farming on the Downs became more intensive, more necessary. The hut was carted out to the fields, where it could act as a base for the shepherd. He had a table, bed and stove – an important part of the equipment, for keeping not only himself warm, but ailing lambs as well. The hut gave him storage for his tools, medicines and his own victuals. It especially came into its own at lambing, when the shepherd might stay in the fields day and night, with his family bringing his meals to him.

There is an illustration in a fourteenth-century manuscript showing a shepherd standing in a wheeled hut, but portable shepherd's huts came into their own in the late eighteenth to early nineteenth century. As they became a standard part of the shepherd's life, their manufacture passed from local carpenters and wheelwrights to bigger firms, who sometimes used corrugated iron instead of wood for the body. Reeves of Bratton, in Wiltshire, was one of them, who made huts in three sizes. By the 1930s sales of new huts were declining: Reeves only sold two in 1930–1, none the next year. Sheep-keeping was changing on the downland hills, reducing the need for shepherd's huts, and there were probably enough old huts to go round, including some second-hand living vans that had been used by steam ploughing or roller crews. Those were palatial compared with the small shepherd's hut. After the Second World War, use of portable homes for the shepherd, especially at lambing, diminished, but has not entirely died out. The shepherd's hut, however, has generally been replaced by a second-hand holiday caravan. Surviving huts, meanwhile, are now valued collector's items.

The literature about shepherds in the early twentieth century made great play of the shepherd's dress. Walter Wooler, one of the Sussex shepherds interviewed by Barclay Wills, for example, was noted as continuing to wear a smock, or 'round frock', which shepherds of the previous century had done. The interest of these writers was probably prompted by the fact that by this time shepherds, in common with most workers on the farm, were ceasing to wear smocks. They might have been useful protection against the grease in the sheep's fleece and proof against a wet day, but an ordinary work suit of cord trousers and tweed jacket was becoming just as practical for most purposes. The late twentieth century saw a move to the new generation of workwear, and the contemporary sheepman strides about in his boiler suit or overalls, bearing the logo of a tractor manufacturer or sheep breed society.

An umbrella of the type used by shepherds on the Downs, in this instance Berkshire. It is a big umbrella to give maximum protection from driving rain, made of blue cotton, with wooden ribs and a turned handle. The apex is reinforced with an extra layer of cotton to prevent rain getting through any gap round the handle. On the handle is a brass ring to hang it up.

Preventing sheep and lambs getting through hedges was a perennial concern for the shepherd. Sometimes he resorted to a shackle, such as this, to link two sheep together. This one was used on a farm in Blackwell, Somerset.

Apart from powered clippers, the shepherd's life has been almost free of mechanisation. He has been one who walked and walked across the fields, with his dogs. He might ride a horse or a motorcycle, but these were not the complete substitute for walking. He could call on horse and wagon to carry hurdles and feed, work latterly taken over by tractor and trailer. The introduction of the all-terrain vehicle – ATV or quad bike – has effected something of a revolution in his work. The shepherd still walks a lot, but also spends time running around on his little vehicle. Honda introduced a three-wheeler in 1970, but this was unstable on rough ground. The four-wheeled versions introduced a few years later were the ones that succeeded. Especially in upland areas, the quad bike has enabled the shepherd to travel the open grazings quickly; even elsewhere they help with moving supplies of feed or taking a few sheep and lambs to new pasture.

A Suzuki quad bike posed for publicity. The sheep were keeping well out of the way.

CONCLUSION:
THE LAST SHEPHERDS?

O NE OF THE THINGS that attracted writers such as Barclay Wills and W. H. Hudson to the old shepherds of the downlands was that their way of life was perceived to be under threat. The sheep-corn husbandry was becoming too expensive to maintain, and by the late 1920s increasing numbers of farmers were abandoning it. If they had sheep on their farms at all, they were often 'flying flocks' brought in for a few months to feed off temporary pasture. Managing these flocks was more akin to ranching than the skills of such as Shepherd Blann. Farmers in these lowland areas were able to dispense with the services of a full-time shepherd, a decision made easier by the fact that it was now becoming difficult to recruit shepherds. Such a lonely and hard occupation was no longer so attractive. This was one reason why some farmers were turning to the national press to advertise for shepherds, although the numbers were few, no more than one or two a week. After the Second World War this trend was reinforced, as the unsocial hours of shepherding proved a real deterrent. The single man, for instance, was finding it difficult to meet a potential partner.

Changes in farm management and pressure on costs have also affected the life of the shepherd in upland Britain. Farmers were not prepared to pay to have shepherds 'studying their sheep': they needed the men to be active on other parts of the farm when the sheep could be left to look after themselves. Sheep are still a major part of the farming scene – numbers of sheep have risen – but the number of flocks has declined. The number of specialist shepherds employed has also declined, as shepherds have had to manage larger flocks over wider areas. Charles Bowden made a study of shepherding life on the Cheviot Hills at the beginning of the twenty-first century, expressing fears that traditional ways of life were threatened. Where once 'every hill had a shepherd on it', one shepherd told him, 'now there's one shepherd to three or four hills.' The outbreak of foot and mouth disease in 2001 had disrupted many shepherding activities, such as shepherds' meets.

However, as long as sheep are kept, they will need attention, and the shepherd's skills will not entirely be lost.